IT
WORKS

THE FAMOUS LITTLE RED BOOK THAT

MAKES YOUR DREAMS COME TRUE!

JEREMY P. TARCHER/PENGUIN
An imprint of Penguin Random House
New York

IT
WORKS

DELUXE EDITION

By R.H.J.

Includes the complete text,
vintage reproduction, and new chapter,
"The Three-Step Miracle: The Story of It Works"
by Mitch Horowitz

JEREMY P. TARCHER/PENGUIN
An imprint of Penguin Random House LLC
375 Hudson Street
New York, New York 10014

Most Tarcher/Penguin books are available at special quantity discounts
for bulk purchase for sales promotions, premiums, fund-raising, and educational
needs. Special books or book excerpts also can be created to fit specific needs.
For details, write: SpecialMarkets@penguinrandomhouse.com.

ISBN 978-0-399-17557-2

Printed in China
3   5   7   9   10   8   6   4

Book design by Gretchen Achilles

CONTENTS

A Definite
Plan of
Accomplishment

SCRIVENER & CO., Publishers
LOS ANGELES, CALIF.

1964

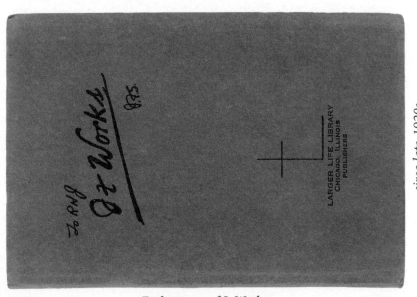

LARGER LIFE LIBRARY
CHICAGO, ILLINOIS
PUBLISHERS

circa late-1920s

Early covers of *It Works*

1966

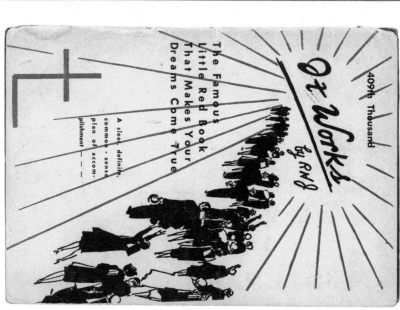

1985

IT
WORKS

THE COMPLETE TEXT

1926

To RHJ

*It Works**

JFS

*The author sent the manuscript of this book for criticism to a friend who returned it with the notation, "It Works." This judgment born of experience was adopted as the title of the book.—*Publishers*

IT
WORKS

All who joy would win must share it,

Happiness was born a twin.

—BYRON

A concise, definite, resultful plan with rules, explanations and suggestions for bettering your condition in life.

If you KNOW what you WANT you can HAVE IT

The man who wrote this book is highly successful and widely known for his generosity and helpful spirit. He gives full credit for all that he has accomplished in mastering circumstances, accumulating wealth and winning friends to the silent working out of the simple, powerful truth which he tells of in his work. He shows you here an easy, open road to a larger, happier life. Knowing that the greatest good comes from helping others without expecting praise, the author of this work has requested that his name be omitted.

WHAT IS THE REAL SECRET OF OBTAINING DESIRABLE POSSESSIONS?

A re some people born under a lucky star or other charm which enables them to have all that which seems so desirable, and if not, what is the cause of the difference in conditions under which men live?

Many years ago, feeling that there must be a logical answer to this question, I decided to find out, if possible, what it was. I found the answer to my own satisfaction, and for years, have given the information to others who have used it successfully.

From a scientific, psychological or theological viewpoint, some of the following statements may be interpreted as incorrect, but nevertheless, the plan has brought the results desired to those who have followed the simple instructions, and it is my sincere belief that I am now presenting it in a way which will bring happiness and possessions to many more.

I f wishes were horses, beggars would ride," is the attitude taken by the average man and woman in regard to possessions. They are not aware of *a power* so near that it is overlooked; so simple in operation that it is difficult to conceive; and so sure in results that it is not made use of consciously, or recognized as *the cause of failure or success.*

G ee, I wish that were mine," is the outburst of Jimmy, the office boy, as a new red roadster goes by; and Florence, the telephone operator, expresses the same thought regarding a ring in the jeweler's window; while poor old Jones, the bookkeeper, during the Sunday stroll, replies to his wife, "Yes, dear, it would be nice to have a home like that, but it is out of the question. We will have to continue to rent." Landem, the salesman, protests that he does all the work, gets the short end of the money and will some day quit his job and find a real one, and President

Bondum, in his private sanctorum, voices a bitter tirade against the annual attack of hay-fever.

At home it is much the same. Last evening, father declared that daughter Mabel was headed straight for disaster, and today, mother's allowance problem and other trying affairs fade into insignificance as she exclaims, "This is the last straw. Robert's school teacher wants to see me this afternoon. His reports are terrible, I know, but I'm late for Bridge now. She'll have to wait until tomorrow." So goes the endless stream of expressions like these from millions of people in all classes who give no thought to what they really want, *and who are getting all they are entitled to or expect.*

If you are one of these millions of thoughtless talkers or wishers and would like a decided change from your present condition, you can have it; but first of all you must *know what you want* and this is no easy task. When you can train your *objective mind* (the mind you use every day) to decide definitely upon the things or conditions you desire, you will have taken your first big step in accomplishing or securing what you know you want.

To get what you want is no more mysterious or uncertain than the radio waves all around you. Tune in correctly and you get a perfect result, but to do this, it is, of course, necessary to know something of your equipment and have a plan of operation.

You have within you a *mighty power*, anxious and willing to serve you, a *power capable* of giving you *that which you earnestly desire.* This power is described by Thomson Jay Hudson, Ph.D., LL.D., author of "The Law of Psychic Phenomena," as your *subjective mind.* Other learned writers use different names and terms, *but all agree that it is omnipotent.* Therefore, I call this Power "Emmanuel" (God in us).

Regardless of the name of this Great Power, or the conscious admission of a God, the Power is *capable and willing* to carry to a complete and perfect conclusion every earnest desire of your objective mind, but you must be really in earnest about what you want.

Occasional wishing or half-hearted wanting does not form a perfect connection or communication with *your omnipotent power.* You must be in earnest, *sincerely* and *truthfully* desiring certain conditions or things—mental, physical or spiritual.

Your objective mind and will are so vacillating that you usually only WISH for things and the wonderful, capable power within you does not function.

Most wishes are simply vocal expressions. Jimmy, the office boy, gave no thought of possessing the red roadster. Landem, the salesman, was not thinking of any other job or even thinking at all. President Bondum knew he had hay fever and was expecting it. Father's business was quite likely successful, and mother no doubt brought home first prize from the Bridge party that day, but they had no fixed idea of what they really wanted their children to accomplish and were actually helping to bring about the unhappy conditions which existed.

If you are in earnest about changing your present condition, here is a *concise, definite, resultful plan, with rules, explanations and suggestions.*

THE PLAN

Write down on paper in order of their importance the things and conditions you really want. Do not be afraid of wanting too much. Go the limit in writing down your wants. Change the list daily, adding to or taking from it, until you have it about right. Do not be discouraged on account of changes, as this is natural. There will always be changes and additions with accomplishments and increasing desires.

THREE POSITIVE RULES OF ACCOMPLISHMENT

1. Read the list of what you want three times each day: morning, noon and night.

2. Think of what you want as often as possible.

3. Do not talk to any one about your plan except to the Great Power within you which will unfold to your Objective Mind the method of accomplishment.

It is obvious that you cannot acquire faith at the start. Some of your desires, from all practical reasoning, may seem positively unattainable, but, nevertheless, write them down on your list in their proper place of importance to you.

There is no need to analyze how this Power within you is going to accomplish your desires. Such a procedure is as unnecessary as trying to figure out why a grain of corn placed in fertile soil shoots up a green stalk, blossoms and produces an ear of corn containing hundreds of grains, each capable of doing what the one grain did. If you will follow this definite plan and carry out the three simple rules, the method of accomplishment will unfold quite as mysteriously as the ear of corn appears on the stalk, and in most cases much sooner than you expect.

When new desires, deserving position at or about the top of your list, come to you, then you may rest assured you are progressing correctly.

Removing from your list items which at first you thought you wanted, *is another sure indication of progress.*

It is natural to be skeptical and have doubts, distrust and questionings, but when these thoughts arise, get out your list. Read it over; or if you have it memorized, talk to your inner self about your desires until the doubts that interfere with your progress are gone. *Remember, nothing can prevent your having that which you earnestly desire.* Others have these things. Why not you?

The Omnipotent Power within you does not enter into any controversial argument. *It is waiting and willing to serve when you are ready*, but your objective mind is so susceptible to suggestion that it is almost impossible to make any satisfactory progress when surrounded by skeptics. Therefore, choose your friends carefully and associate with people who now have some of the things you really want, but *do not discuss your method of accomplishment with them.*

Put down on your list of wants such material things as money, home, automobile, or whatever it may be, but do not stop there. Be more definite. If you want an automobile, decide *what kind, style, price, color,* and all the other details, including *when* you want it. If you want a home, plan the structure, grounds and furnishings.

Decide on location and cost. If you want money, write down the amount, If you want to break a record in your business, put it down. It may be a sales record. If so, write out the total, the date required, then the number of items you must sell to make it, also list your prospects and put after each name the sum expected. This may seem very foolish at first, but you can never realize your desires if you do not *know positively and in detail what you want and when you want it.* If you cannot decide this, you are not in earnest. You must be definite, and when you are, results will be surprising and almost unbelievable.

A natural and ancient enemy will no doubt appear when you get your first taste of accomplishment. This enemy is Discredit, in form of such thoughts as: "It can't be possible; it just happened to be. What a remarkable coincidence!"

When such thoughts occur *give thanks and assert credit to your Omnipotent Power* for the accomplishment. By doing this, you gain assurance and more accomplishment, and in time, prove to yourself that *there is a law, which actually works—at all times—*when you are in tune with it.

Sincere and earnest thanks cannot be given without gratitude and it is impossible to be thankful and grateful without being happy. Therefore, when you are thanking your greatest and best friend, *your Omnipotent Power*, for the gifts received, do so *with all your soul, and let it be reflected in your face.* The Power and what it does is beyond understanding. Do not try to understand it, but *accept the accomplishment* with thankfulness, happiness, and strengthened faith.

CAUTION

It is possible to want and obtain that which will make you miserable; that which will wreck the happiness of others; that which will cause sickness and death; that which will rob you of eternal life. You can have what you want, but you must take all that goes with it: so in planning your wants, *plan that which you are sure will give to you and your fellow man the greatest good here on earth; thus paving the way to that future hope beyond the pale of human understanding.*

This method of securing what you want applies to everything you are capable of desiring and the scope being so great, it is suggested that your first list consist of only those things with which you are quite familiar, such as an amount of money or accomplishment, or the possession of material things. Such desires as these are more easily and quickly obtained than the discontinuance of fixed habits, the welfare of others, and the healing of mental or bodily ills.

Accomplish the lesser things first. Then take the next step, and when that is accomplished, you will seek the higher and really important objectives in life, but long before you reach this stage of your progress, many worthwhile desires will find their place on your list. One will be to help others as you have been helped. *Great is the reward to those who help and give without thought of self, as it is impossible to be unselfish without gain.*

IN CONCLUSION

A short while ago, Dr. Emile Coué came to this country and showed thousands of people how to help themselves. Thousands of others spoofed at the idea, refused his assistance and are today where they were before his visit.

So with the statements and plan presented to you now. You can reject or accept. You can remain as you are or *have anything you want.* The choice is yours, but God grant that you may find in this short volume the inspiration to choose aright, follow the plan and thereby obtain, as so many others have, all things, whatever they may be, that you desire.

(see next page)

Read the entire book over again, *and again*, AND THEN AGAIN.

Memorize the three simple rules on pages seventeen and eighteen.

Test them now on what you want most *this minute.*

This book could have extended easily over 350 pages, but it has been deliberately shortened to make it easy as possible for you to read, understand and use. Will you try it? Thousands of bettered lives will testify to the fact that *It Works.*

IT WORKS! TESTIMONIALS

"Please send another 200 copies of *It Works!* In answer to your query, yes, we are obviously using it(!) and yes, we think it's simply great."

Carol-Ann Atkinson
Tri-State Marketing Research
Overland Park, KS

"*It Works!* has been a proven training adjunct at Shawmut-Bridges Equities for almost a decade."

Kevin Griffin
Shawmut-Bridges Equities
Boston, MA

"We now require use of *It Works!* in the first month of all OAS and OAS Services training."

(Lt. Col.) Clark North
OAS INTEL
Reston, VA

"Since using *It Works!* in our agent training program, we have noticed a dramatic increase in motivation and performance, and a steady surge in sales that bucks all the downtrends. Please keep it in print."

Stacy York, Vice President
Pan-Desert Realtors Association
Palm Springs, CA

"I was given *It Works!* in training fourteen years ago and I now require it for training in all Broadmart Centers."

Rick Windsor
Broadmart Sales & Training
San Francisco, CA

"Terrific! Thanks! We've used it for years, and it really *does* work."

Harley Tillman
First Capital Stock & Equity
Silver Springs, MD

A LETTER TO YOU
FROM THE AUTHOR

Dear Reader:

The great possessions of life are all GIFTS mysteriously bestowed: sight, hearing, aspiration, love or life itself.

The same is true of ideas—the richest of them are given to us, as for instance, the powerful idea which this book has given you. What are you going to do with it? Are you surprised when I tell you the most profitable thing you can do is to give it away?

You can do this in an easy and practical way by having this book sent to those you know who NEED IT. In this way, you can help in the distribution of this worthwhile effort to make the lives of others better and happier.

You know people who are standing still or who are worried and discouraged. This is your chance to HELP

THEM HELP THEMSELVES. If you withhold this book from them you will lose the conscious satisfaction that comes from doing good. If you see that they get this book, then you put yourself in line with the Law of Life which says, "You get by giving," and you may rightly expect prosperity and achievement.

At the very least you will have the inner sense of having done a good deed with no hope of being openly thanked and your reward will come secretly in added power and larger life.

THE AUTHOR

IT
WORKS

VINTAGE

REPRODUCTION

CIRCA MID-1930S

*The following is a photographic reproduction
of an early edition of It Works, exactly as it
appeared during the author's lifetime.*

To RHJ

It Works

.75.

A Definite
Plan of
Accomplishment

LARGER LIFE LIBRARY
BEVERLY HILLS, CALIF.
PUBLISHERS

It Works

All who joy would win must share it,
Happiness was born a twin.
                                    —BYRON.

Send "It Works" to Your Friends

To RHJ

*It Works**

JFS

Single Copy 50 Cents

*The author sent the manuscript of this book for criti-
cism to a friend who returned it with the notation,
"It Works." This judgment born of experience was
adopted as the title of the book.—*Publishers.*

TENTH PRINTING

PRINTED AND DISTRIBUTED BY
DEVORSS & CO.
843 SOUTH GRAND AVENUE
LOS ANGELES, CALIFORNIA, U. S. A.

A concise, definite, resultful
plan with rules, explanations
and suggestions for bettering
your condition in life.

If you KNOW what you
WANT you can HAVE IT

The man who wrote this book is highly successful
and widely known for his generosity and helpful
spirit. He gives full credit for all that he has
accomplished in mastering circumstances, accumulating wealth and winning friends to the silent
working out of the simple, powerful truth which
he tells of in this work. He shows you here an
easy, open road to a larger, happier life. Knowing that the greatest good comes from helping
others without expecting praise, the author of
this work has requested that his name be omitted.

*What is the real secret of
obtaining desirable possessions?*

ARE some people born under a
lucky star or other charm which
enables them to have all that which
seems so desirable, and if not, what
is the cause of the difference in conditions under which men live?

Many years ago, feeling that there
must be a logical answer to this question, I decided to find out, if possible,
what it was. I found the answer to
my own satisfaction, and for years,
have given the information to others
who have used it successfully.

From a scientific, psychological or
theological viewpoint, some of the

following statements may be interpreted as incorrect, but nevertheless, the plan has brought the results desired to those who have followed the simple instructions and it is my sincere belief that I am now presenting it in a way which will bring happiness and possessions to many more.

"IF wishes were horses, beggars would ride," is the attitude taken by the average man and woman in regard to possessions. They are not aware of *a power* so near that it is overlooked; so simple in operation that it is difficult to conceive; and so sure in results that it is not made use of consciously, or recognized as *the cause of failure or success.*

It Works

"GEE, I wish that were mine", is the outburst of Jimmy, the office boy, as a new red roadster goes by; and Florence, the telephone operator, expresses the same thought regarding a ring in the jeweler's window; while poor old Jones, the bookkeeper, during the Sunday stroll, replies to his wife, "Yes, dear, it would be nice to have a home like that, but it is out of the question. We will have to continue to rent." Landem, the salesman, protests that he does all the work, gets the short end of the money and will some day quit his job and find a real one, and President Bondum, in his private sanctorum, voices a bitter tirade against the annual attack of hay-fever.

It Works

At home it is much the same. Last evening, father declared that daughter Mabel was headed straight for disaster, and today, mother's allowance problem and other trying affairs fade into insignificance as she exclaims, "This is the last straw. Robert's school teacher wants to see me this afternoon. His reports are terrible, I know, but I'm late for Bridge now. She'll have to wait until tomorrow." So goes the endless stream of expressions like these from millions of people in all classes who give no thought to what they really want, *and who are getting all they are entitled to or expect.*

If you are one of these millions of thoughtless talkers or wishers and

It Works

would like a decided change from your present condition, you can have it; but first of all you must *know what you want* and this is no easy task. When you can train your *objective mind* (the mind you use every day) to decide definitely upon the things or conditions you desire, you will have taken your first big step in accomplishing or securing what you know you want.

To get what you want is no more mysterious or uncertain than the radio waves all around you. Tune in correctly and you get a perfect result, but to do this, it is, of course, necessary to know something of your equipment and have a plan of operation.

It Works

You have within you a *mighty power*,
anxious and willing to serve you, a
power capable of giving you *that which
you earnestly desire.* This power is
described by Thomson Jay Hudson,
Ph.D., LL.D., author of "The Law
of Psychic Phenomena" as your *subjective mind.* Other learned writers use
different names and terms, *but all agree
that it is omnipotent.* Therefore, I call
this Power, "Emmanuel" (God in us).

Regardless of the name of this Great
Power, or the conscious admission of
a God, the Power is *capable and willing* to carry to a complete and perfect conclusion every earnest desire of
your objective mind, but you must
be really in earnest about what you

It Works

want. Occasional wishing or half-
hearted wanting does not form a perfect connection or communication
with *your omnipotent power.* You must
be in earnest, *sincerely* and *truthfully*
desiring certain conditions or things,
mental, physical or spiritual.

Your objective mind and will are so
vacillating that you usually only WISH
for things and the wonderful, capable
power within you does not function.

Most wishes are simply vocal expressions. Jimmy, the office boy, gave
no thought of possessing the red roadster. Landem, the salesman, was not
thinking of any other job or even
thinking at all. President Bondum

knew he had hay fever and was expecting it. Father's business was quite likely successful and mother no doubt brought home first prize from the Bridge party, that day, but they had no fixed idea of what they really wanted their children to accomplish and were actually helping to bring about the unhappy conditions which existed.

If you are in earnest about changing your present condition, here is a *concise, definite, resultful plan, with rules, explanations and suggestions.*

It Works

THE PLAN

WRITE down on paper in order of their importance the things and conditions you really want. Do not be afraid of wanting too much. Go the limit in writing down your wants. Change the list daily, adding to or taking from it, until you have it about right. Do not be discouraged on account of changes, as this is natural. There will always be changes and additions with accomplishments and increasing desires.

THREE POSITIVE RULES OF ACCOMPLISHMENT

1. *Read the list of what you want three times each day: morning, noon and night.*

2. *Think of what you want as often as possible.*

3. *Do not talk to any one about your plan except to the Great Power within you which will unfold to your Objective Mind the method of accomplishment.*

It is obvious that you can not acquire faith at the start. Some of your desires, from all practical reasoning, may seem positively unattainable; but, nevertheless, write them down on your list in their proper place of importance to you.

There is no need to analyze how this Power within you is going to accomplish your desires. Such a procedure

It Works

is as unnecessary as trying to figure out why a grain of corn placed in fertile soil shoots up a green stalk, blossoms and produces an ear of corn containing hundreds of grains, each capable of doing what the one grain did. If you will follow this definite plan and carry out the three simple rules, the method of accomplishment will unfold quite as mysteriously as the ear of corn appears on the stalk, and in most cases much sooner than you expect.

When new desires, deserving position at or about the top of your list, come to you, then you may rest assured you are progressing correctly.

It Works

Removing from your list items which at first you thought you wanted, *is another sure indication of progress.*

It is natural to be skeptical and have doubts, distrust and questionings, but when these thoughts arise, get out your list. Read it over; or if you have it memorized, talk to your inner self about your desires until the doubts that interfere with your progress are gone. *Remember, nothing can prevent your having that which you earnestly desire.* Others have these things. Why not you?

The Omnipotent Power within you does not enter into any controversial argument. *It is waiting and willing to*

It Works

serve *when you are ready*, but your objective mind is so susceptible to suggestion that it is almost impossible to make any satisfactory progress when surrounded by skeptics. Therefore, choose your friends carefully and associate with people who now have some of the things you really want, but *do not discuss your method of accomplishment with them.*

Put down on your list of wants such material things as money, home, automobile, or whatever it may be, but do not stop there. Be more definite. If you want an automobile, decide *what kind, style, price, color,* and all the other details, including *when* you want it. If you want a home, plan

the structure, grounds and furnishings.
Decide on location and cost. If you
want money, write down the amount.
If you want to break a record in your
business, put it down. It may be a
sales record. If so, write out the total,
the date required, then the number
of items you must sell to make it,
also list your prospects and put after
each name the sum expected. This
may seem very foolish at first, but
you can never realize your desires if
you do not *know positively and in detail what you want and when you want
it*. If you can not decide this, you
are not in earnest. You must be definite, and when you are, results will
be surprising and almost unbelievable.

It Works

A natural and ancient enemy will no doubt appear when you get your first taste of accomplishment. This enemy is Discredit, in form of such thoughts as: "It can't be possible; it just happened to be. What a remarkable coincidence!"

When such thoughts occur *give thanks and assert credit to your Omnipotent Power* for the accomplishment. By doing this, you gain assurance and more accomplishment, and in time, prove to yourself that *there is a law, which actually works—at all times—* when you are in tune with it.

Sincere and earnest thanks can not be given without gratitude and it is

impossible to be thankful and grateful without being happy. Therefore,
when you are thanking your greatest
and best friend, *your Omnipotent
Power,* for the gifts received, do so *with
all your soul, and let it be reflected in
your face.* The Power and what it does
is beyond understanding. Do not try
to understand it, but *accept the accomplishment* with thankfulness, happiness
and strengthened faith.

CAUTION

*It is possible to want and obtain that
which will make you miserable; that which
will wreck the happiness of others; that
which will cause sickness and death; that
which will rob you of eternal life.* You
can have what you want, but you

It Works

must take all that goes with it: so in planning your wants, *plan that which you are sure will give to you and your fellow man the greatest good here on earth; thus paving the way to that future hope beyond the pale of human understanding.*

This method of securing what you want applies to everything you are capable of desiring and the scope being so great, it is suggested that your first list consist of only those things with which you are quite familiar, such as an amount of money or accomplishment, or the possession of material things. Such desires as these are more easily and quickly obtained than the discontinuance of fixed habits, the welfare of others and the healing of mental or bodily ills.

Accomplish the lesser things first. Then take the next step, and when that is accomplished, you will seek the higher and really important objectives in life, but long before you reach this stage of your progress, many worth while desires will find their place on your list. One will be to help others as you have been helped. *Great is the reward to those who help and give without thought of self, as it is impossible to be unselfish without gain.*

It Works

IN CONCLUSION

A short while ago, Dr. Emil Coué came to this country and showed thousands of people how to help themselves. Thousands of others spoofed at the idea, refused his assistance and are today where they were before his visit.

So with the statements and plan presented to you now. You can reject or accept. You can remain as you are or *have anything you want*. The choice is yours, but God grant that you may find in this short volume the inspiration to choose aright, follow the plan and thereby obtain, as so many others have, all things, whatever they may be, that you desire.   *(See next page)*

It Works

Read the entire book over again, *and again*, AND THEN AGAIN.

Memorize the three simple rules on pages thirteen and fourteen.

Test them now on what you want most *this minute.*

This book could have extended easily over 350 pages but it has been deliberately shortened to make it as easy as possible for you to read, understand and use. Will you try it? Thousands of bettered lives will testify to the fact that *"It Works"*.

A Letter to You from the Author

Dear Reader:

The great possessions of life are all GIFTS mysteriously bestowed: sight, hearing, aspiration, love or life itself.

The same is true of ideas—the richest of them are given to us, as for instance, the powerful idea which this book has given you. What are you going to do with it? Are you surprised when I tell you the most profitable thing you can do is to give it away?

You can do this in an easy and practical way by having this book sent to those you know who NEED IT. In this way, you can help in the distribution of this worth-while effort to make the lives of others better and happier.

This is your chance to HELP OTHERS HELP THEMSELVES. If you withhold this book from them you will lose the conscious satisfaction that comes from doing good. If you see that they get this book, then you put yourself in line with the Law of Life which says, "You get by giving," and you may rightly expect prosperity and achievement.

At the very least you will have the inner sense of having done a good deed and your reward will come in added power and larger life.

THE AUTHOR.

(Use order on next page or write a letter)

The Meaning of the Mark

By the Author of "IT WORKS"

*Satisfies your desire for more
advanced knowledge and
greater mastery of conditions.*

Paul Omar, a successful business man, seemed to possess the ancient magic of the East in fulfilling his desires. His power, which was apparently unlimited, resided in the application of a philosophy summed up in the simple but significant design or mark of mystery which was his symbol and guide.

The secret of the meaning of this mark, the reason for its power and the way to use it are clearly revealed for the first time in this absorbing book.

"The Meaning of the Mark" contains a tale big with the romance of achievement. It gives you a philosophy for a successful life, so clear and simple that anyone can use it. Replete with incidents and examples demonstrating the effect and value of this great success sign. "The Meaning of the Mark" shows you how the things that CAN'T be done ARE done.

Second Edition, with Introduction and Author's Foreword, 168 pages. Price $1.50.

THE THREE-STEP MIRACLE:

THE STORY OF *IT WORKS*

BY MITCH HOROWITZ

You must know what you want
before you can ask for it.
—NEVILLE GODDARD, Prayer

The little book called *It Works*, written in 1926 by an anonymous Chicago salesman, is one of the most deceptively simple yet seismically powerful statements to emerge from the American metaphysical scene of the twentieth century.

In the early decades of the century, a wide range of spiritual writers, social reformers, and mystical ministers experimented with and articulated a philosophy often called New Thought. Their outlook centered on one key idea: *thoughts are causative.*

This notion—that what you think shapes reality—so deeply entered American life after the Second World War that it could no longer be considered the property of any one movement, but became a kind of national creed, best known through the title of Norman Vincent Peale's 1950s landmark *The Power of Positive Thinking.*

This was the culture that gave birth to *It Works.* Within the first edition's twenty-eight pages there appeared an almost unthinkably simple but alluring three-step exercise: 1) make a list of your truest desires and read it morning, noon, and night; 2) think about your list as often as possible; and 3) tell no one about what you're doing.

Then watch your wishes come true—and duly express thanks.

That's it? What reasonable person could believe, much less attempt, such a rudimentary, even childish, method to achievement? Indeed, most detractors didn't try it—and never came to understand why the little book won the affection of more than a million readers over the course of nearly a century, making *It Works* one of the most popular, if below-the-radar, books of spiritual self-help.

The "secret" to *It Works* is that it compels us to do something we think that we do all the time but, in actuality, rarely try: come to terms with *what we really want.* We certainly *believe* that we know what we want. We constantly tell ourselves *I'd like to buy that, work there, date him,* and so on. But we rarely, if ever, sit down in a sustained and self-revealing way, stripped of all conformities and prejudices, and lay bare our truest, most absolute desires.

We may or may not want to act on those desires—there may be costs and burdens, ethical or otherwise. There may be unforeseen consequences or compromises. But, just as often, we harbor within us a true, noble, and altogether sound life direction that we never articulate or attempt. This is because we are so continually distracted by the chitter-chatter in our heads that we almost never stop—completely stop—to ask: *What do I really want?*

And there may be more to the "simple" formula in this little book than just that. The clarified, motivated mind may also possess an agency that we have not yet fully reckoned with in modern Western life, but that is indicated in placebo studies, neuroplasticity, quantum enigmas, and psychical research. There may be unacknowledged mental properties and possibilities that this three-step program sets in motion, or at least hints at. To get at that deeper question requires going back to where it started: Chicago in the early twentieth century—and the origin of *It Works.*

EVERYMAN PHILOSOPHER

In the 1920s, as today, some social critics believed that New Thought's law-of-attraction theology bred selfishness by encouraging material acquisition. One New Thought figure of the day sought to resolve the moral quandaries of self-seeking metaphysics. He wanted to devise a philosophy of achievement that also encouraged ethical growth and inner refinement. He concealed his identity behind the initials R.H.J.—this was Roy Herbert Jarrett.

By profession, Jarrett sold typewriters and office printing machines. But this salesman accomplished what few practical philosophers or ministers ever did: He constructed a morally grounded philosophy of personal success and higher living, couched in everyday, immensely persuasive language. At age fifty-two, Jarrett brought his ideas to the world through his self-published, pocket-sized pamphlet *It Works.*

Ordinary Americans who may have heard something about the new metaphysics and its promises of personal power, wealth, and peace of mind now had a way to test such claims by reading R.H.J.'s pamphlet in the space of an average lunch break. And many did. Readers who had never before given much notice to metaphysical ideas bought, and often gave away, large numbers of *It Works,* sending grateful testimonials to the address that Jarrett provided inside his reprints of the little book.

As indicated by his title, Jarrett intended *It Works* to be *useful.* According to the legend recounted at the front of the pamphlet, Jarrett had originally sent his short manuscript to a friend for critique. He identified this individual only by the initials J.F.S. The friend returned it with the simple notation "IT WORKS," which Jarrett opted to use on his cover.

As it happens, the legend is true. The friend was Jewell F. Stevens, owner of an eponymous Chicago advertising agency, which specialized in religious books and items. In 1931, Stevens hired Jarrett to join his agency as a merchandising consultant and account manager. For Jarrett, the new position was deliverance from a tough, working-class background and years of toil in the Willy Loman domain of sales. Jarrett became the example of his own success philosophy.

A PILGRIM'S PROGRESS

Like many early purveyors of New Thought, Roy Herbert Jarrett came from difficult roots. The man who affixed his initials to *It Works* was born in 1874 to a Scottish immigrant household in Quincy, Illinois. His father worked as an iceman and a night watchman. Jarrett's mother died when he was eight. By his mid-twenties, Jarrett was married and living in Rochester, New York, working as a sales manager for the Smith Premier Typewriter Company. His first marriage failed, and by 1905 he returned to the Midwest to marry a new wife and live closer to his elderly father. In Chicago, Jarrett found work as a salesman for the American Multigraph Sales Company. It was the pivotal move of his life.

American Multigraph manufactured typewriters and workplace printing machinery. In a sense, the company was the Apple Computer of its day. Its flagship product, the Multigraph, was an innovative, compact printing press. The device took up no more space than an office desk and could be operated without specialized knowledge. The Multigraph was the first generation of such easy-to-use presses, allowing offices to produce their own flyers, mailers, and newsletters. American Multigraph had a reputation in the printing trade for its gung ho culture and pep rally sales conventions. And the manufacturer possessed a sense of mission.

"For years," wrote the industry journal *Office Appliances*

in September 1922, "a feature of every convention has been an address on 'The Romance of the Multigraph' by Advertising Manager Tim Thrift." On the surface, Thrift told salesmen, the Multigraph could print labels, newsletters, and pamphlets. But one must peer into "the soul of what to some appears as a machine." The Multigraph, he said, was "not a thing of metal, wood and paint; a mere machine sold to some man who can be convinced he should buy it. Ah, no! The Multigraph is a thing of service to the world . . ."

Cynics could laugh, but for Roy Jarrett the company's motivational tone, combined with the magic-seeming efficiency of modern printing, helped launch him on the idea of *It Works.*

Jarrett's belief in inspirational business messages dovetailed with his interest in autosuggestion and mental conditioning. Such ideas reached Jarrett through the work of a French pharmacist and self-taught psychologist named Emile Coué, who had visited Chicago. Jarrett's vision grew from a cross-pollination of American business motivation and the ideals of the French mind-power theorist.

STRONGER EVERY DAY

Born in Brittany in 1857, Emile Coué developed an early interest in hypnotism, which he pursued through a mail-order course from Rochester, New York. Coué more rigorously studied hypnotic methods in the late 1880s with physician Ambroise-Auguste Liébeault. French therapist Liébeault was one of the founders of the so-called Nancy School of hypnotism, which promoted its therapeutic uses.

While working as a pharmacist at Troyes, in northwestern France, in the early 1900s, Coué made a startling discovery: Patients responded better to medications when he spoke in praise of the formula. (This same insight was replicated in a 2014 Harvard Medical School placebo study of migraine medications.) Coué came to believe that the imagination aided not only in recovery but also in a person's general sense of well-being. From this theory, Coué developed a method of "conscious autosuggestion." It was a form of waking hypnosis that involved repeating confidence-building mantras while in a relaxed or semi-conscious state.

Coué argued that many people fail to meet their potential in life due to a poor self-image. Our *willpower*, or drive to achieve, he said, is constantly overcome by our *imagination*, by which he meant a person's unconscious self-perceptions. "When the will and the imagination are opposed to each other," he wrote, "it is always the *imagination* which *wins . . .*" By way of example, he asked people to think of walking across a wooden plank laid on the floor—obviously, an easy task. But if the same plank is elevated high off the ground, the task becomes fraught with fear even though the physical demand is the same. This, Coué asserted, is what we are constantly doing on a mental level when we *imagine* ourselves as worthless or weak.

Coué's method of *autosuggestion* was a model of simplicity. He told patients to repeat the mantra: *Day by day, in every way, I am getting better and better.* It was to be recited twenty times each morning and each evening, just loud enough to hear, while lying in bed upon awakening and before going to sleep, with eyes closed and the mind focused on what you desire. He advised using a string with twenty knots to count off the repetitions, as if saying rosary beads.

In the early 1920s, news of Coué's method reached America. The "Miracle Man of France" briefly grew into an international sensation. American newspapers featured Ripley's Believe It or Not!–styled drawings of Coué, looking like a goateed magician and gently displaying his knotted string at eye level like a hypnosis device. In early 1923, Coué made a three-week lecture tour of America. One of his final stops was in Jarrett's hometown in February, where the Frenchman delivered a talk at Chicago's Orchestra Hall.

In a raucous scene, a crowd of more than two thousand demanded that the therapist help a paralytic man, who had been seated on stage. Coué defiantly told the audience that his autosuggestive treatments could work only on illnesses that originated in the mind. "I have not the magic hand," he insisted. Nonetheless, Coué approached the man and told him to concentrate on his legs and to repeat "It is passing . . . It is passing." The seated man struggled up and haltingly walked. The crowd exploded. Coué rejected any notion that his "cure" was miraculous and insisted that the man's disease must have been psychosomatic.

To some American listeners, Coué's message of self-affirmation held special relevance for oppressed people. The pages of Marcus Garvey's newspaper, *Negro World,* echoed Coué's day-by-day mantra in the headline "Every Day in Every Way We See Drawing Nearer and Nearer the Coming of the Dawn for Black Men." The paper editorialized that Garvey's teachings provided the same "uplifting psychic influence" as Coué's.

Coué took a special liking to Americans. He found American attitudes a refreshing departure from what he knew back home. "The French mind," he wrote, "prefers first to discuss and argue on the fundamentals of a principle before inquiring into its practical adaptability to every-day life. The American mind, on the contrary, immediately sees the possibilities of it, and seeks . . . to carry the idea further even than the author of it may have conceived."

The therapist could have been describing the salesmanseeker Roy Jarrett. "A short while ago," Jarrett wrote in 1926, the year of Coué's death, "Dr. Emile Coué came to this country and showed thousands of people how to help themselves. Thousands of others spoofed at the idea, refused his assistance and are today where they were before his visit." But Jarrett saw the potential.

Taking his cue from the ease of Coué's approach, Jarrett devised "Three Positive Rules to Accomplishment" in *It Works*. In summary, they went:

1. Carefully write a list of what you really want in life— once you are satisfied with it, read it three times daily: morning, noon, and night.

2. Think about what you want as often as possible.

3. Keep your practice and desires strictly to yourself. (This was intended to prevent other people's negative reactions from sullying one's inner resolve.)

Just as Coué had observed about American audiences, Jarrett boldly expanded on the uses of autosuggestion. In the steps of the American metaphysical tradition, Jarrett believed that training the subconscious did more than recondition the mind. It activated a divine inner power that served to out-picture a person's mental images into the surrounding world. "I call this power 'Emmanuel' (God in us)," Jarrett wrote.

The notion of writing down one's desires also struck a chord with motivational pioneer Napoleon Hill, who embraced the method in his 1937 self-help classic *Think and Grow Rich.* Hill believed that writing down a concrete list could serve to influence the subconscious mind. Once the subconscious became impressed with a central aim or idea, he taught, its subliminal forces would function as a kind of homing device that would bring us in touch with people, circumstances, ideas, and situations that would aid in the achievement of our goals.

"After you have accepted, as a reality, the existence of your subconscious mind, and understand its possibilities, as a medium for transmuting your DESIRES into their physical or monetary equivalent," Hill wrote—with capitalized emphasis in the original—"you will also understand why you have been repeatedly admonished to MAKE YOUR DESIRES CLEAR, AND TO REDUCE THEM TO WRITING."

A STRIVER'S LEGACY

Self-published under the imprint of the Larger Life Library, Jarrett's pamphlet quickly won an audience and ran through multiple printings. Many readers swore by it and wrote in for additional copies to give away to friends (something Jarrett encouraged with a bulk-order form). But he felt incomplete. It wasn't that he chafed at using mind-power for material ends—indeed, Jarrett urged readers to use *It Works* for money, career advancement, or just about anything they wanted. But he believed that many had missed the book's deeper point. "Merely giving you the simple rules to accomplishment, with brief instructions as to their use," he wrote several years later, "while beneficial, is not satisfying."

Jarrett's deeper purpose in *It Works* was only hinted

at by a mysterious symbol he placed on its cover. Below the title appeared a simple drawing of a cross, with its foot curving at a right angle, in a square. The square-and-cross appeared on every copy of the little red pamphlet until 1992, when a later publisher removed it. (It has been restored to this edition.) That symbol, wrote Jarrett's friend Stevens, "was really the undisclosed reason for the book."

What was this beguiling square-and-cross, which some readers ignored, some wondered about, and a publisher later cut? Five years after producing *It Works,* Roy Jarrett made a little-known and final foray into publishing. In 1931, he produced a thoughtful and ambitious work, *The Meaning of the Mark.* This longer volume served as an inner key to *It Works*—it explained his strange symbol and dealt directly with the moral quandaries of success-based spirituality.

Jarrett said that the square-and-cross was his personal symbol of spiritual awakening. Its meaning, he hoped, would be intuitively felt by readers. The square represented earthly values, particularly the need to treat others with the respect one seeks for oneself, which he saw as the hidden key to achievement. But there was another part to the matter. Personal attainment could find its lasting and proper purpose only when conjoined to the cross—the presence of God. Together, individual striving and receptivity to the Divine would bring man into the fullness of life. Jarrett wrote:

> The definition of correct thinking for our purpose is: "thoughts which are harmoniously agreeable to God and man as a whole." Thoughts agreeable to God come to you through the intuitive messages from your soul, often intensified by the senses. Thoughts agreeable to man come to you more frequently through the senses and are often intensified by intuition.

By dwelling on the meaning of the square-and-cross, he reasoned, the reader could be constantly reminded to unite the two currents of life.

The success of *It Works* helped Jarrett attain a lifestyle that, while not extravagant, went beyond anything his laborer father could have hoped for. Jarrett and his wife retired to a sunny, hacienda-style bungalow in a tidy section of Beverly Hills. But their California idyll was fated to be short-lived. Jarrett died there in 1937 at age sixty-three from leukemia. He had been diagnosed three years earlier.

Roy Herbert Jarrett didn't embark on his career as a writer until the final years of his life. He produced both of his books while in his fifties. His success arose not *despite* the lateness of his start but *because* of it. Like the best New Thought pioneers, this self-educated man from ordinary life devised a philosophy that had been tested by the nature of his own personal conduct and lived experience. Only then did he deem it worth sharing.

MITCH HOROWITZ is vice president and editor in chief at Tarcher/Penguin, and the PEN Award–winning author of *Occult America* and *One Simple Idea: How Positive Thinking Reshaped Modern Life*, in which parts of this essay first appeared. Visit him at MitchHorowitz.com.

ABOUT THE AUTHOR

ROY HERBERT JARRETT (1874-1937), aka R.H.J., was a Chicago sales executive and advertising man. After many years of studying metaphysical success methods, Jarrett produced his landmark pamphlet *It Works* in 1926. It has since sold more than 1.5 million copies. In 1931 Jarrett followed up his mind-power classic with his second and final book, *The Meaning of the Mark*, which served as the "inner key" to his earlier volume. It is available in a rediscovery edition from Tarcher/Penguin.

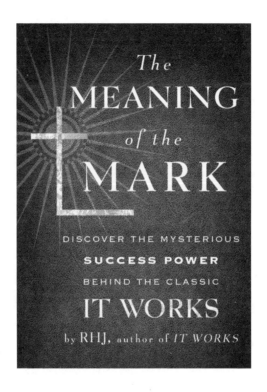

The MEANING of the MARK

DISCOVER THE MYSTERIOUS **SUCCESS POWER** BEHIND THE CLASSIC

IT WORKS

by RHJ, author of *IT WORKS*

The inner key to *It Works* and the author's expanded vision . . . Discover a lost classic, *The Meaning of the Mark*, now in a beautiful reissue edition from Tarcher/Penguin.